SPOTLIGHT ON
AN EQUITABLE SOCIETY

STEPPING UP
AS AN ALLY

Mary Ratzer

ROSEN
PUBLISHING

Published in 2025 by The Rosen Publishing Group, Inc.
2544 Clinton Street, Buffalo, NY 14224

Editor: Greg Roza
Book Design: Michael Flynn

Photo Credits: Cover Halfpoint/Shutterstock.com; cover, p. 3 (hands) Dedraw Studio/Shutterstock.com; (series Earth icon) v4ndhira/Shutterstock.com; p. 5 Rawpixel.com/Shutterstock.com; p. 6 Matt Gush/Shutterstock.com; p. 7 Margoe Edwards/Shutterstock.com; p. 8 Julie Clopper/Shutterstock.com; p. 9 Jan H Andersen/Shutterstock.com; p. 11 https://commons.wikimedia.org/wiki/File:NAACP_leaders_with_poster_NYWTS.jpg; p. 13 Sundry Photography/Shutterstock.com; p. 14 Motortion Films/Shutterstock.com; p. 15 Africa Studio/Shutterstock.com; p. 17 CarlosBarquero/Shutterstock.com; p. 18 https://commons.wikimedia.org/wiki/File:Front_entrance_of_Sylvan_Hills_High_School.jpg; p. 19 Simon Drayton/Shutterstock.com; p. 21 Lopolo/Shutterstock.com; p. 22 oneinchpunch/Shutterstock.com; p. 23 Eli Wilson/Shutterstock.com; p. 25 Halfpoint/Shutterstock.com; p. 26 Ground Picture/Shutterstock.com; p. 27 Dmytro Zinkevych/Shutterstock.com; p. 29 Krakenimages.com/Shutterstock.com.

Cataloging-in-Publication Data

Names: Ratzer, Mary Boyd.
Title: Stepping up as an ally / Mary Ratzer.
Description: Buffalo, NY : Rosen Young Adult, 2025. | Series: Spotlight on an equitable world | Includes glossary and index.
Identifiers: ISBN 9781499477320 (pbk.) | ISBN 9781499477191 (library bound) | ISBN 9781499477030 (ebook)
Subjects: LCSH: Belonging (Social psychology)--Juvenile literature. | Respect for persons--Juvenile literature. | Interpersonal relations--Juvenile literature.
Classification: LCC BF723.B45 R38 2025 | DDC 155.2--dc23

Manufactured in the United States of America

Some of the images in this book illustrate individuals who are models. The depictions do not imply actual situations or events.

CPSIA Compliance Information: Batch #CSRYA25. For further information contact Rosen Publishing at 1-800-237-9932.

Find us on

CONTENTS

Chapter One

MEET AN ALLY

Let me introduce you to an ally. You have known this person for a long time, or maybe they just showed up to help. This ally can be old or young, tall or short, confident or shy. The ally has the awareness to know when to step up and doesn't look the other way. Unlike those who don't care, the ally chooses to act. Unlike all the others who run to watch a fight or join in verbal abuse, the ally shows up to encourage, assist, defend, listen, and care.

With empathy, allies care about others who need support. The ally is the one who says, "Why are you doing that?" to a bully pushing someone around. With little recognition for being an ally, this person feels that standing up is its own reward. Living with values and beliefs that motivate them to act, the ally risks getting backlash from the people they stand up to. The ally is part of solutions and learns from experience.

Seeking others who are like minded, the ally brings strengths and talents to a collaborative effort to help those in need. Seeking fairness, the ally is an active citizen who speaks up and communicates with decision-makers. Seeking solutions, the ally works with others to solve problems, not in hopes of receiving a trophy. The ally gets relationships, positive change, and satisfaction in knowing they made a constructive impact on society.

Does this description of what an ally is and does sound familiar? Can you identify the allies in your life?

Chapter Two

WITH ALLIES, WITHOUT ALLIES

A lyric from a popular song is: "Lean on me when you're not strong . . . I'll help you carry on." At some point you have needed allies. At some point in your life, you have been an ally. With allies, so much is possible even in very hard times. Without allies, there are fewer possibilities there for you.

With allies you have the strength and talent of many. You have the combined problem-solving skills of those who want to make things better. You have support and empathy. You have resources beyond your own. You have people who share your challenges. When difficult situations seem impossible to resolve, you have hope.

Watch the news any day. Allies are responding to a crisis somewhere. Think about disastrous flooding in hard-hit states.

SANDBAGS

Allies in a flooded neighborhood chip in to help their neighbors recover.

Widespread flooding cut off towns from rescue crews and washed out roads and homes. Days of downpours caused damage usually seen in floods only every 1,000 years. People died. Others were trapped without water, phone service, or electricity.

Help came from strangers in the form of hundreds helicopter rescuers and swift water boat rescues. Soldiers in the National Guard stepped up. Food, water, and shelter needs received immediate response from community members. Charitable organizations launched disaster relief efforts. Volunteers removed waterlogged belongings, floors, and sheetrock from flooded homes. Tractor trailers from many sources arrived with supplies and equipment. Neighbors who lost everything still helped neighbors.

What do you think would happen if a disaster such as this one struck your community, and no one arrived to help?

Chapter Three

EQUITY AND FAIRNESS FOR ALL

Can you be an ally for social justice? You learn about social justice from experiences, role models, and a growing awareness of the real world beyond your family. Your potential as an active citizen depends on developing character, skills, understanding, and personal attitudes. This kind of learning leads to actions and values that are needed for social justice to progress.

How do you achieve social justice in sixth grade, seventh grade, or high school? By familiarizing yourself with social justice concepts and history, you can prepare yourself to identify instances of injustice and work to fix them.

This memorial in West Potomac Park, Washington, D.C., depicts Martin Luther King Jr. King gave so much in his pursuit of civil rights for all—including his life.

An understanding of social justice takes effort and empathy.

The following "I know" statements are based on the National Social Justice Standards (created by the Southern Poverty Law Center). Think about how these real-world targets would result in achieving social justice.

- I know about some of the people, groups, and events in the history of social justice and the ideas and beliefs that affected them.
- I can understand stereotypes about groups of people and see them around me.
- I consider people to be individuals.
- I can identify injustice in many forms including attitudes, words, behaviors, laws, practices, and institutions.
- I understand that biased words, actions, and laws limit the rights and freedoms of people because of their identity.
- I know that where people are born and who they are result in advantages and disadvantages.

Chapter Four

SOCIAL JUSTICE AND ALLIES

Think about what you already know about social justice in the United States. Progress in social justice is still a work in progress. How has positive change opened fair access to opportunities, resources, and human rights? One force making progress is alliances where many people come together to make change happen.

In 1963, 250,000 united people marched for jobs and freedom in Washington, D.C. They heard the Rev. Martin Luther King Jr. deliver his "I Have a Dream" speech. As a leader of the Civil Rights Movement, King spoke of the future he was fighting for. His inspiring words influenced Presidents John F. Kennedy and Lyndon B. Johnson to work for change.

For the 100 years after the Emancipation Proclamation of 1863 declared that enslaved people in the United States were free, there was little progress ending racism in the country. The words of King and the march influenced the Civil Rights Act of 1964. The act prohibited discrimination. It strengthened the enforcement of voting rights and the desegregation of schools. The Voting Rights Act of 1965 and other laws opened access to opportunities and human rights. Despite these efforts, achieving social justice remains a challenge today.

A collaboration of strong allies with common goals brought together the quarter million marchers. They got the attention of the American people and the nation's leaders. The following allies helped change history.

This photograph from 1956 shows four leaders of the NAACP at the time: from left to right, Henry L. Moon, Roy Wilkins, Robert Hill, and future Supreme Court Justice Thurgood Marshall.

- **Congress of Racial Equality (CORE)**
- **Southern Christian Leadership Conference (SCLC)**
- **John Lewis, Student Nonviolent Coordinating Committee (SNCC)**
- **Brotherhood of Sleeping Car Porters**
- **National Association for the Advancement of Colored People (NAACP)**
- **National Catholic Conference for Interracial Justice**
- **Commission on Race Relations of the National Council of Churches**
- **American Jewish Committee**
- **Labor Unions UAW & AFL-CIO**

Chapter Five

UNFINISHED WORK

In 1920, when the 19th Amendment gave women the right to vote, women of color living in the South and West faced barriers to voter registration and couldn't vote. The suffrage movement was originally allied with Frederick Douglass, a leader for the rights of Black Americans. Southern officials expressed the concern that white men's votes would be outnumbered by those of Black women. With the racist culture in the south, Black women had to fight longer to finally be able to vote.

Allies again shaped the effort for voting rights for Black women, but this time the allies were focused to find ways to overcome the roadblocks built by prejudice. Voting rights in the South are still actively in jeopardy. Since 2020, 19 states have passed laws that limit the right to vote, and 440 bills to limit voting were proposed in state legislatures. This is called voter suppression. By eliminating early voting, voting by mail, and registration on the day of an election, many poor and Black voters are pushed out of their right to vote. Requirements for voting as in the past are intended to make it very difficult for young, old, and poor voters.

In some states all voting rolls have been eliminated and voters must start from scratch to register. Intentionally holding back information about where and how to register to vote or to cast a vote is a major barrier to social justice. Women allies from across the United States sent millions of cards and letters to southern voters about where and how to register and vote.

STOP VOTER SUPPRESSION AND GERRYMANDERING WE DEMAND SAFE SECURE ELECTIONS 4 ALL

Voter suppression is a big hurdle to social justice today. So is gerrymandering, which is the unfair practice of dividing election districts in a way that gives one political party an advantage over other political parties.

Chapter Six

DECIDING TO BE AN ALLY

Deciding to be an ally might be a quick response to a sudden event. Bullies trip a student in the hall. Books and papers fly everywhere. Bystanders think this is funny and laugh. Your empathy motivates you to step up and intervene. You take a risk but stand by your values. Reacting to an incident can be the way many people are inspired to become allies.

Decisions about being an ally are often challenging. Since standing up for others in need often involves risks, some decide to be a bystander instead. However, if you decide to keep yourself safe instead of intervening, you can follow up by seeking help from an adult. Talking to someone in private about a problem can still get results without being as stressful.

Have you ever been a witness to someone being bullied in school? What did you do?

Responding to a need is the way many become community allies. This response can be sudden or active for a long time. For example, in many towns, allies work together every summer to provide food for children who depend on school lunch. Working with churches and community groups, allies share the responsibility and the effort. Allies respond when sudden weather events damage homes and property. Allies welcome refugees and support their needs.

Some towns organize days of service. Many allies come forward to contribute in a variety of ways including community cleanups and planting trees. Schools sponsor community give-back days, and children engage in volunteer projects. Service and social connections with fellow allies can be rewarding. In this way, volunteers become a dedicated part of the solutions to problems.

Chapter Seven

REFLECT, PRACTICE, GROW

Like learning to skateboard, cook, play an instrument, or dive off a diving board, being an ally requires some skill. Learning to be an ally takes some guidance and time. As you try your own skills you can reflect on what seems to work and begin to put together your tools for action. Practice helps you to refine strategies and build confidence.

Organizations in schools and communities, such as the National Coalition Building Institute, can provide willing students with training. In some communities, businesses sponsor these programs and support them with funds, meeting spaces, and encouragement. One such organization is Right to Be. The group's model for learning, featured in books and training videos, includes the five Ds: distract, delegate, document, delay, and direct.

Each skill empowers a bystander to act if a situation is hurtful. Distracting a bully or a target works in many settings. Delegating means turning the problem over to a trusted adult to act. Document means take responsibility to capture the who, what, where, and when of a problem that is happening. Use that information to report the facts and get a response. Delay means following up with a person targeted by a bully and offering help and support. Direct means to speak up, intervene, or act to stop a situation. Many allies will confirm that some bullies are not that tough and will quit their negative action if one or two allies confront them.

Standing up for peers who are being bullied can be scary, but there's always something you can do to help and show you care. Most importantly, tell an adult about the situation so something can be done about it.

Chapter Eight

ALLIES STEP UP

Teen and adolescent allies are a part of uplifting news stories every day. They accomplish amazing things and prove their power to make positive change. A wakeup call can inspire a person to respond to a problem close to home. They can channel their empathy and take action to make a difference.

In 2023, tornadoes leveled the town of Sherwood, Arkansas. Members of the Sylvan Hills High School football team and their coach volunteered to help in the cleanup effort. They went house to house with water and supplies and helped move debris and fallen trees. This was payback for the community that supports them. Offensive tackle Josh Lawrence said, "It's just great to help the community out and show them that we are a brotherhood and we're willing to help anybody out."

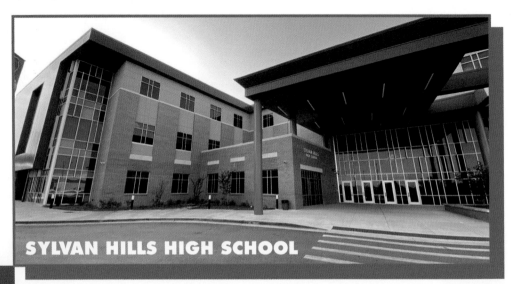

SYLVAN HILLS HIGH SCHOOL

Tornadoes are destructive forces that can cause a lot of damage to a community. Allies can help make the destruction a positive force for good. How would you help?

In other schools, allies have stepped up in meaningful ways to support classmates stricken with cancer or other life-threatening illnesses. Whole schools have joined together to support and encourage very sick kids. Peers facing the challenge of hospitalization, side effects from treatment, and physical limitations need all the allies they can get.

Cancer is stressful, and being bald in middle school makes it worse. In many schools, when this happens, allies work together to raise this person up with empathy. Sometimes all the kids on a team or in a class cut their hair and let their peer know they stand with them. This takes a lot of courage.

How could a group of kids work together as allies to solve a problem? The answers are up to you.

Chapter Nine

INVISIBLE ALLIES

Motivated by compassion and the power to help others, many allies are invisible heroes. Watch for them; they might be close by. Like a matching game, these allies put together a need with a solution. Alone, the job might be too hard. Together, each shared success is a victory.

A bike is an important part of self-esteem, freedom, and social connections for young people. Free Bikes for Kids is just one source of generous support for children without bikes. About 100,000 volunteers and more than 700 companies are working together to find, restore, purchase, and donate 1 million bikes by 2027. Neighborhood allies have replaced broken or stolen bikes for children who need support, but they are often invisible allies.

In a small town, a handicapped veteran spent time in a small diner and got around with a motorized scooter. One day the veteran didn't show up for coffee. It took two days for the invisible allies to discover that his scooter had broken down. It took two more days for allies to raise over $3,000 for a new scooter that "just appeared" on the veteran's front yard.

In one celebrity foundation, Look to the Stars, successful musical performers have gathered allies to bring music education to schools without resources. These talented allies knew that music education could create a path to success for disadvantaged children. Creative self-expression and personal discipline as part of this program allows young people to let their talents shine. Schools receive the funds to buy instruments and teach music to all students.

Owning a bicycle gives young people a sense of independence and self-esteem. But what about children whose families can't afford a bicycle?

Chapter Ten

STAND BY ME

Allies excel in showing solidarity. Showing solidarity means you would stand with others in a time of need. As the slang expression goes, you "do a solid" for a person or a group.

Starting with teens your age, what does solidarity look like? It's all around you, but there is no big neon sign flashing "Solidarity Here." Young people stand by their friends in solidarity. They might stand by shelter animals and work to make their lives better. Solidarity with a community action project often involves children. The summer reading program in an eastern state encouraged kids to pick up and recycle plastic in solidarity with the ocean. If a classmate experiences an illness or if their family has a crisis, students can stand by them in creative and supportive ways.

People, companies, and governments all over the world have supplied Ukraine with resources to help them survive warfare in their own country. Others have joined protests.

Many people in the United States stand in solidarity with those whose rights are violated or who suffer injustice. They might walk in a protest march or assist in other ways. Military men and women stand by each other. Soldiers recovering from wounds or post-traumatic stress disorder are rarely alone. Workers stand together seeking fairness and safety. When a shortage of baby formula for allergic infants struck because of supply problems, thousands of women stood by moms and babies in need. Solidarity is a powerful force in making positive change and showing visible support.

Nations stand by other nations in solidarity with their needs. Many countries of the world stand in solidarity with Ukraine and its people. Global response to famine, disasters, refugees, and disease is international solidarity.

Chapter Eleven

CHANGING SCHOOL CULTURE

Bad things can happen when good people fail to step up to help others. When a school culture is uncaring, unsafe, or negative, students often don't want to be there. They aren't motivated to succeed. They have poor relationships with peers and teachers. Just walking down the hall could be stressful. Without a safe, positive, inclusive environment, people struggle.

What if students in your school were harassing certain ethnic groups or damaging the building? What if they're filming themselves wrecking bathrooms for clout on TikTok? What if they set off fire alarms as a prank? What if there are fights between individuals or groups that other kids rush to see? What if kids aren't engaged with meaningful learning? What if good people did nothing about this culture?

When change is absolutely the only option, good people need to do something. When facing hate and harm, young people can say with determination, "Not in my school!" They can create opportunities for peace, respectful relationships, conflict resolution, and community building. Young people who want to affect change can start by modeling care and empathy. They can bring people together by taking advantage of their unique strengths and keeping in mind the needs of each member of the school community. They can raise awareness and start the move toward progress.

Convincing good people to be part of the solution can be helpful. Those who have the will to be allies just need a way to connect with those who are visibly striving for positive change.

Together, allies can work to improve the culture of their school. This experience can help allies move beyond school and help others in their community and around the world.

Chapter Twelve

ALLIES CHANGE A SCHOOL

When students have difficulty forming relationships with teachers who care, those students are likely to struggle. Schools can respond to this need by matching students with an ally who is part of the staff and school community. Building a relationship, the student/ally pair stay connected. When students find someone they trust, they can build a relationship. Mentors are powerful allies and can be older students or even community members. A student can change their outlook and quality of school life by taking the time to check in and problem-solve with their mentor.

Determined allies can change a school culture. They can organize service opportunities to help the community and persuade good people to connect. Open mic nights shine a light on diverse

Many school teachers, counselors, and coaches are happpy to provide guidance and support. All you have to do is ask.

talents and bring young people together. Panel discussions with student participants and experts educate young people about things that put them at risk. These can be followed up with opportunities for those who need support.

Student allies can promote their mission by communicating about kindness and respect. Morning meetings bring students together and fosters open conversations. People can share good will by carrying out random acts of kindness. What if students brought coffee to the parking lot security guy or cookies to a room where students had to stay for test prep after school?

Tougher actions might include getting adults involved. Allies can share what might be hurtful with a trusted teacher. Does someone have a dangerous plan? Did kids see or hear a threat? Are kids harassing someone who is different? Together, an alliance of good people, including trusted adults, can and do change a school community for the better.

Chapter Thirteen

SMALL STEPS, BIG DIFFERENCE

Some young people, such as the 16 teens suing the state of Montana for violating their right to a healthy community, are environmental superhero allies. Millions of young people working for the environment in small and effective ways have powers of their own. Maybe unseen and yet dedicated to action, kids who care about their future can be role models for everyone. Young people have inspired families, schools, and communities to solve problems for the environment.

Have you ever heard the phrase "Think globally, act locally"? If you pick up trash and recycle the plastic or cans you find, the planet is a little bit healthier because of you. If you unplug electronics in your house that stay on and use energy, you're saving the energy produced by fossil fuels. Walk or bike to destinations close by and the air in your town benefits. If you conserve water, the planet is just a bit more sustainable. If you recycle, reuse, or repurpose, you are reducing solid waste.

Buying local food and eating less meat reduces greenhouse gases. Long-distance trucking of food and the methane produced by cattle warm the planet. Use refillable water bottles instead of disposable ones. Give up paper cups and plates. Turn down the heat in winter to use less energy. Do something that reverses food waste in your school cafeteria. Those uneaten tater tots add up! Plant a tree. Join a community clean up. The power to make a big difference with small steps is right at your fingertips. This is your planet.

Using a refillable water bottle, rather than buying water sold in plastic water bottles, is a simple way to contribute to the health of the planet.

Chapter Fourteen

PICTURING ALLIES

Look around. Like a game of I Spy, watch for allies. Recognize their presence in your community and your world. Draw conclusions about who they are and what they do. Think about what is possible because of them. Remember them. Seek inspiration from them. Imagine yourself among them.

Let's say you are riding to school, and you see a girl with her seeing-eye dog walking confidently to the library. A stranger is helping an older man who has a flat tire by the side of the road. Your bus driver greets every kid with a smile. Volunteers are arriving at the church kitchen down the street to prepare lunch for their 120 homeless regulars. The local grocery store dropped off day-old baked goods and some produce. The mayor is working on a Code Blue Shelter Plan that provides a warm space for homeless people when cold weather comes.

The school nurse is helping a girl who has a fever. Outside the cafeteria the Parent Teacher Association has set up a small free store that includes a rack of winter coats and new sneakers. The coach talks to your class about a faculty versus student basketball game to benefit a student who needs help with medical bills. Who will volunteer?

Volunteers are teaching English to newly arrived immigrants at the community center. Your mom is giving a neighbor a ride to a medical appointment. Your dentist is running a free clinic once a month.

Be aware of allies around you. They could inspire you to step up and be an ally too.

GLOSSARY

backlash: A strong negative reaction by a large number of people.

bias: To have an unfair preference or dislike of something.

collaborate: To work together with others to reach a common goal.

desegregation: To end by law the isolation of members of a particular race in separate units/schools.

discrimination: The treating of some people better than others without any fair or proper reason.

empathy: Being aware of and sharing another person's feelings, experiences, and emotions.

inclusive: Not excluding people from something.

institution: An established organization or corporation and especially one of a public nature.

intervene: To come between in order to stop, settle, or change a situation.

mentor: To teach, give guidance, or give advice to someone, especially a less experienced person.

potential: Capable of becoming real.

PTSD: Short for post-traumatic stress disorder; a condition triggered by a traumatic event, resulting in anxiety, fear, nightmares, and more.

stereotype: An unfair and often untrue belief about someone or a group of people.

suppression: The act of suppressing (stopping) an activity.

volunteer: Offer to do something for free.

INDEX

TITLES IN THIS SERIES

ROSEN
PUBLISHING

ISBN: 9781499477320

9 781499 477320